My Forever Friend

FAMILY HOME
CHRISTIAN BOOKS
www.FamilyHomeChristianBooks.com

www.FamilyHomeChristianBooks.com

Original text from *The Desire of Ages* by E. G. White

Cover Design by David Berthiaume
Text Design by Greg Solie • AltaGraph

ISBN: 978-1-5136-0031-4

My Forever Friend

The stories in this book are—

The Best Gift

This story is taken from Matthew 1, Luke 1,
and *The Desire of Ages,* chapter 1.

When God created the world, everything was perfect. Everyone was happy.

Lions played with lambs. Bears made friends with bunnies. Snakes were not slithery and scary like they are now, but beautiful creatures that flew in the air.

God completed His world by creating a man and a woman. Adam and Eve loved their garden home. And they loved to walk and talk with God every day.

He told them, "You can enjoy all the things in this garden except one: Do not eat any fruit from this tree."

But one day an awful thing happened. Satan pretended to be a colorful snake. He hid in that tree and called out, "Eat some yummy fruit from this tree! You don't have to obey God!"

Eve and Adam listened to Satan and ate the fruit. Then everything changed. Everything broke.

The animals became scared. They were not friendly anymore. And the flowers and plants began to die.

Now Adam and Eve would die too. And they could not live in the garden with God anymore.

It was very, very sad.

For thousands of years, Satan ruled this world. Most people did not know that God cared about them. They just tried to survive in a broken, lonely world.

But God had a plan. He would send His Son Jesus to earth to show us how much we are loved.

One day a girl named Mary got a surprise visitor. It was an angel!

This angel, named Gabriel, said, "Hello! God has chosen you for a very special job."

Mary felt scared and amazed. "What job could this be?" she wondered.

The angel told Mary, "You are going to be the mother of a baby Boy. He will be the Son of God."

"The Son of God?" Mary must have asked. Her eyes opened wide.

"Yes. Don't be afraid," the angel said. "God is very pleased with you. That is why He has chosen you."

Mary bowed down on her knees. Then she said a beautiful thing: "I am the Lord's servant. May God's will be done in my life."

How amazing. The Son of God would be born as a little baby, just like you.

Mary was going to marry a good man named Joseph. So God sent an angel to Joseph, too.

"Joseph, do not be afraid to take Mary to be your wife," the angel told him.

Joseph wondered if he was dreaming.

"Mary's Baby is from the Holy Spirit," Gabriel said. "You are to give Him the name Jesus. He will save His people."

Joseph nodded. "The Holy Writings said this would happen," he agreed.

He knew the prophecy. It said: "Behold, the virgin shall conceive and bear a Son, and you shall call His name Immanuel," which means "God with us."

And that is what Jesus was—God with us. He was the best gift ever given!

Jesus' Birthday

This story is taken from Luke 2 and *The Desire of Ages*, chapter 4.

Mary and Joseph felt very tired. They had been traveling all day. The sun was setting and painting the sky with beautiful colors.

Joseph's feet hurt from walking so far. Mary rode on a donkey hour after hour. *Bounce, bounce* went the donkey. *Bounce, bounce* went Mary. How she longed to lie down on a soft bed!

The ruler, Caesar Augustus, had said that everyone must travel to the place where they were born. He wanted to count the people in his empire. Then he could make them pay him money called taxes.

As Mary and Joseph walked through the gates of Bethlehem the moon rose high in the sky and the stars began to shine. Crowds of people bumped into them. Joseph had to lead the donkey out of the way.

"Wait here, Mary," Joseph told his wife. "I will find a place for us to sleep."

But there were no empty beds. All of them were filled with people. Joseph could not find a spot in any house or inn where his tired wife could rest.

Finally one innkeeper said, "You can sleep in my stable."

People did not stay in stables. Only animals did! Mary had to share a bedroom with cows, donkeys, and chickens. There was clucking and snorting and loud chewing.

Mary could not go to sleep. She felt pains that told her this would be the night her Baby would be born.

There were no doctors there to make sure everything turned out all right. There were no clean hospital sheets to make Mary more comfortable. And there were no medicines to help the pain.

But God's Son was born on earth that night.

Mary wrapped her Baby in pieces of cloth. Then she laid Him in a manger. That was a feedbox with hay in it where the animals ate. What a beginning for the Savior of the world!

If the innkeeper or any of the people who turned Mary and Joseph away could have known who they were, and who the Baby would become, surely they would have made room for them. But that is the way it is in this world sometimes. People do not listen for the voice of God to tell them to be kind to others.

22

Meanwhile, out on the hills surrounding Bethlehem, shepherds watched over their flocks of sheep. It was a cold night. They sat close to the fire as they talked about the promises in Scripture of a Messiah.

Suddenly a bright light made them blink their eyes. A mighty angel stood among them. His face shone like the sun.

"I have good news that is going to bring this world great happiness," he said. "Tonight, right here in Bethlehem, a Savior has been born who is Christ the Lord."

The shepherds had been waiting for Him. So they ran to find Jesus and worship Him!

What a Boy

This story is taken from Luke 2 and
The Desire of Ages, chapter 9.

Nazareth was not the best place for a child to grow up. People in the other towns made fun of it. They said, "Can any good thing come out of Nazareth?"

But this little mountain village in Galilee became home for the Son of God. He was not raised in a palace. He passed by the houses of the rich. He grew up among the poor, common people.

Yet anyone would have been blessed to have Him living near them.

What was a normal day like for Jesus as a boy? He started His mornings studying the Scriptures with His mother. Maybe He sat on her lap as she taught Him how to read the Bible for Himself. He also memorized verses that would help Him during His life. And can't you hear them singing songs together?

The Bible tells us, "Jesus increased in wisdom and stature, and in favor with God and men." That means He grew taller. He grew wiser. He pleased the people around Him. He also pleased God, His Father in heaven.

In the afternoons Jesus helped His earthly father, Joseph, in the carpenter shop. There Jesus learned to work with His hands. He learned to build things out of wood. The sounds of hammers and saws echoed in the shop as Jesus helped make tables, chairs, and yokes for oxen.

Nature was His teacher too. Jesus loved to go out in the hills and fields around His home. He knew all of the plants and animals. After all, He had helped create them four thousand years before!

Jesus always started His day in prayer. It was prayer that helped Him be kind to His brothers, who did not believe He was the Messiah. Prayer gave Him courage to share His lunch with someone who had nothing to eat. And prayer helped Him understand that He had come to this world for a very special reason.

Jesus was human, and He was God. Satan tried to get Jesus to sin and do wrong. But Jesus never disobeyed God. He used the Scriptures to help Him do what was right. When Satan tempted Him, He would answer "It is written …" and recite Bible passages.

Jesus was God with all the power in the universe to create worlds. Yet He never used this power to help Himself.

He left the golden throne in heaven. He left the angels, who were happy to do anything for Him.

He came as a baby. He grew up as a boy. And He learned to trust in God just as you and I do.

He understands what we go through. He was willing to go through the same troubles. We should be glad that He loved us that much!

Wash Me

This story is taken from Matthew 3, Mark 1, Luke 3, John 1, and *The Desire of Ages*, chapter 11.

John the Baptist was Jesus' cousin. God gave him the important job of telling people that Jesus was coming.

John went to live in the dessert. There he studied the Scriptures and prayed. He did not have much to eat except grasshoppers and honey. His clothes were made of camel's hair.

He told the people, "The Messiah is coming! Ask for forgiveness for the things you have done wrong. Be baptized to wash away your sins!"

People came from the city and faraway towns to hear his message.

They asked him, "Who are you? Are you the Christ?"

"I am not the Christ," John replied.

"Are you the prophet?" they asked.

"No," John told them. "I am the voice of one calling in the wilderness, 'Prepare the way for the Lord.'"

Some of the religious leaders did not like what John said. But many of the people asked, "If we have done wrong, how can we make it right?"

"If you have two shirts, give one to someone who has none," John said. "And if you have food, share it."

Many people listened to
John. They wanted their sins
forgiven. They wanted to become
kinder and more loving. They
wanted to be ready for Jesus to
come.

So they asked to be baptized.
They would go down under the
water and come back up. That
would show they were starting a
new life.

"I baptize you with water,"
John said. "But One mightier
than I is coming, whose sandal
strap I am not worthy to loose.
He will baptize you with the Holy
Spirit."

One day John saw Jesus
coming toward him. John said,
"Behold! The Lamb of God who
takes away the sin of the world!"

The crowds looked. All they saw was an ordinary man dressed in simple clothing. Jesus stepped down into the river with John. He asked to be baptized.

"How can this be?" John wondered. "Jesus has no sins to wash away. Why is He asking me to baptize Him?"

John said to Jesus, "Are You coming to me? I need to be baptized by You!"

"We need to set an example for others," Jesus explained. "It is only right that we do this to fulfill the prophecies of the Scriptures."

So John baptized Jesus. When Jesus came up out of the water, He bowed in prayer on the riverbank.

Suddenly it seemed as though the sky opened. A white dove came down and landed on Jesus. It was really the Holy Spirit.

God's voice from heaven said, "You are My beloved Son; in You I am well pleased."

We can choose to follow Jesus too. And we can be baptized to show that we love Him. There is joy in heaven every time someone makes a decision to let Jesus guide their life.

Through the Roof

This story is taken from Matthew 9, Mark 2, Luke 5, and *The Desire of Ages*, chapter 27.

One day Jesus was teaching in the home of Simon Peter. Peter was one of Jesus' closest followers, called a disciple. The house was packed with guests.

Suddenly everyone heard a noise overhead. *Scratch, scratch.* Something was up on the roof. Maybe it was a bird or an animal.

Bang, bang! The noises got louder. No bird could make that noise!

Everyone looked up at the ceiling. Dirt fell down in their faces.

Thud! Slam! Crack! A part of the roof opened up. Rays of sunlight flashed through the falling dust.

"Who is up there?" Peter shouted. He peered through the hole in his ceiling.

Whack! Wham! Now a piece of clay fell to the floor right by Jesus.

"What are you doing to my house?" we can hear Peter shouting again.

There was no answer from above. But now the hole in the roof was big.

Bash! Smash! More noises sounded. Then something came down from the roof.

It was a hammock held up by cords of rope. Men on the roof lowered the hammock and set it down in front of Jesus.

48

In the hammock lay a man. He looked thin and sick. He could not move.

His friends looked down from the roof. They hoped Jesus would heal him. They had heard many stories about Jesus making sick people well.

They had tried to come in the door. But they could not squeeze through the crowd. So they broke a hole in the roof!

The man in the hammock just lay there. He looked at Jesus.

The crowd moved back. They watched the man. They watched Jesus.

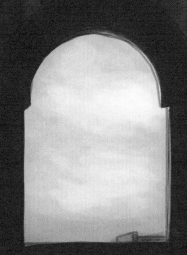

Jesus bent down by the man's side. He looked into his eyes with kindness.

"Man, your sins are forgiven," Jesus said. He knew what the man needed to hear the most.

A look of peace came over the sick man's face. His crippled arms and legs seemed to relax.

Jesus turned to him again. "But that you may know that the Son of Man has power on earth to forgive sins," Jesus commanded, "I say to you, arise, take up your bed, and go to your house."

The sick man's eyes opened wide. He leaned forward as if to take Jesus at His word. Then he stood to his feet.

He got a big smile on his face. His friends cheered.

The crowd shouted praises for this miracle. A few minutes ago this man could not walk. Now he was jumping up and down! He was singing in joy!

He was all better. And his sins were forgiven.

We too can have a clean heart. All we have to do is ask Jesus.

Sinking Boat

This story is taken from Matthew 8, Mark 4, Luke 8,
and *The Desire of Ages*, chapter 35.

One evening Jesus and His twelve disciples got in Peter's boat. Together they pushed the boat off from shore. Then they raised the sails.

Swoosh! Soon the sails waved in the breeze.

They wanted to cross the Sea of Galilee. People called it a sea, but it was really a large lake.

As it got dark, the men looked up at the twinkling stars. Maybe they watched a half-moon rise in the sky.

Then the wind grew stronger. *Howl! Whip!* The disciples looked up at the sky. The stars had disappeared behind big clouds.

It began to rain. Huge drops of water blew into the eyes of the disciples. Their clothes became soaked.

Boom! Clap! Crash! Thunder sounded. Then lightning split the sky with bright light.

The boat rocked and swayed. *Whip! Whack!* The sails looked like they would rip in the strong wind.

"We better take down the sails!" Peter shouted.

The disciples grabbed oars to get the boat under control. But rowing seemed useless.

The wind and waves were so wild! The lightning and thunder were so scary! It was as if the storm was some giant monster.

Another huge wave washed over the side of Peter's boat. *Splash!* The disciples tried bailing out the water, but more kept washing in. *Swish! Splash!*

"Our boat is sinking!" the disciples cried.

Suddenly they thought of Jesus. Where was He?

They looked around the boat. He was sleeping soundly in the back of the boat! Didn't He know they were in a big storm? Didn't He know they were scared? Didn't He know they were in danger? Their boat was ready to sink!

Then another wave hit Peter's boat. It almost flipped over.

Everybody screamed, "Help us, Lord! Don't You care if we die?"

Jesus woke up. Quickly He grabbed the swaying mast of Peter's boat. For a moment He stared into the night sky. Then He shouted above the screeching wind and crashing waves, "Peace! Be still!"

The storm obeyed His voice! The wind stopped. The rain stopped. The thunder stopped. The lightning stopped. The waves grew still. The clouds went away.

The half-moon appeared again. Then the stars came out. It was amazing!

The disciples could not believe it. They whispered among themselves, "Who can this be that even the winds and the sea obey Him?"

But Jesus was disappointed with His disciples. "Why were you afraid?" He asked them sadly. "Have I been with you this long, and still you are afraid?"

The disciples had much to learn. Maybe the greatest lesson was that when Jesus was with them, they did not need to fear anything.

That is a lesson for us today. Jesus is always with us, and He hears our prayers.

Miracle Girl

This story is taken from Matthew 9, Mark 5, Luke 8, and *The Desire of Ages*, chapter 36.

One day a man named Jairus hurried up to Jesus. He was a leader in Capernaum.

"Master!" he called. "My little daughter is dying. Please come and put Your hands on her. Then she will be healed and live."

The doctors had not been able to help. Jesus was his only hope.

"Take Me to your daughter," Jesus said.

The ruler's house was not far away. But crowds of people pressed around Jesus. He could not move fast.

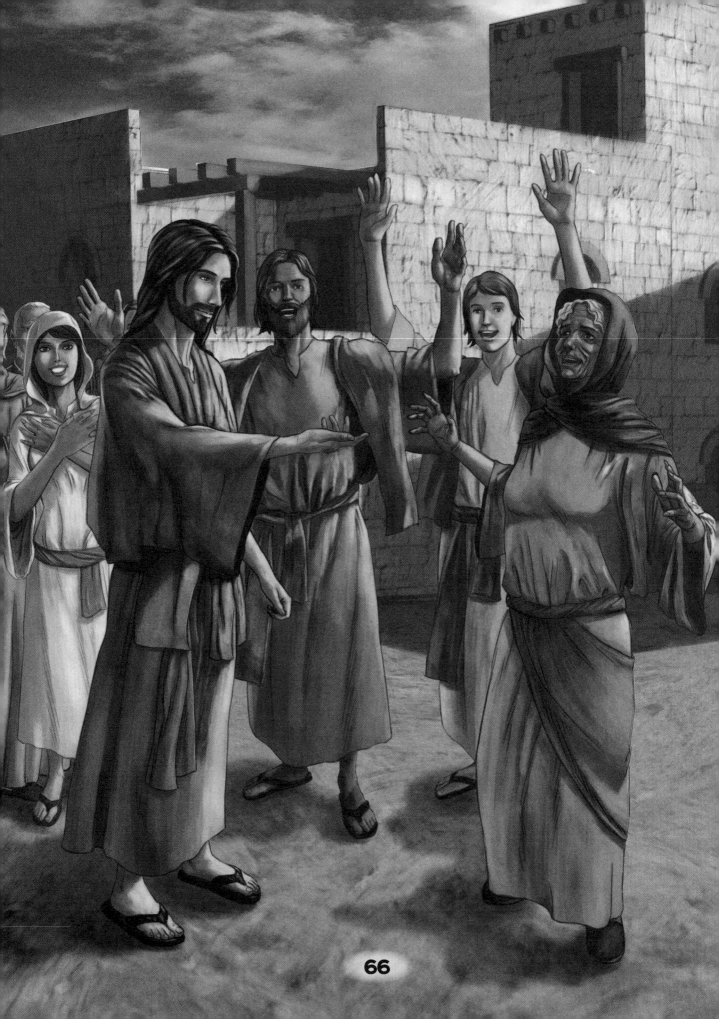

Then Jesus stopped along the way. An old woman needed healing. She had been sick for many years.

After Jesus healed her, she praised God. Everyone around her clapped and celebrated.

But then a messenger arrived. He had bad news to give Jairus.

"Your daughter is dead," the messenger said. "Do not trouble the Teacher."

"No! Please! This cannot be true!" Jairus sobbed.

Jesus heard what they were saying. "Do not be afraid," He said to Jairus. "Only believe, and your little girl will be made well."

Jesus kept walking until He reached Jairus' house. Relatives and hired mourners filled the house with their groaning and wailing. Waaah! Sob! Sniffle.

"Step aside, please," Jesus said. "She is not dead. She is only sleeping."

Jesus walked into the girl's room. He invited only a few people to go with Him. Her mother and father came. So did His closest disciples, Peter, James, and John.

Jesus took the girl's hand. He raised His eyes to heaven. "Little girl, get up!" He said.

The little girl opened her eyes. She sat up. Then she jumped to her feet.

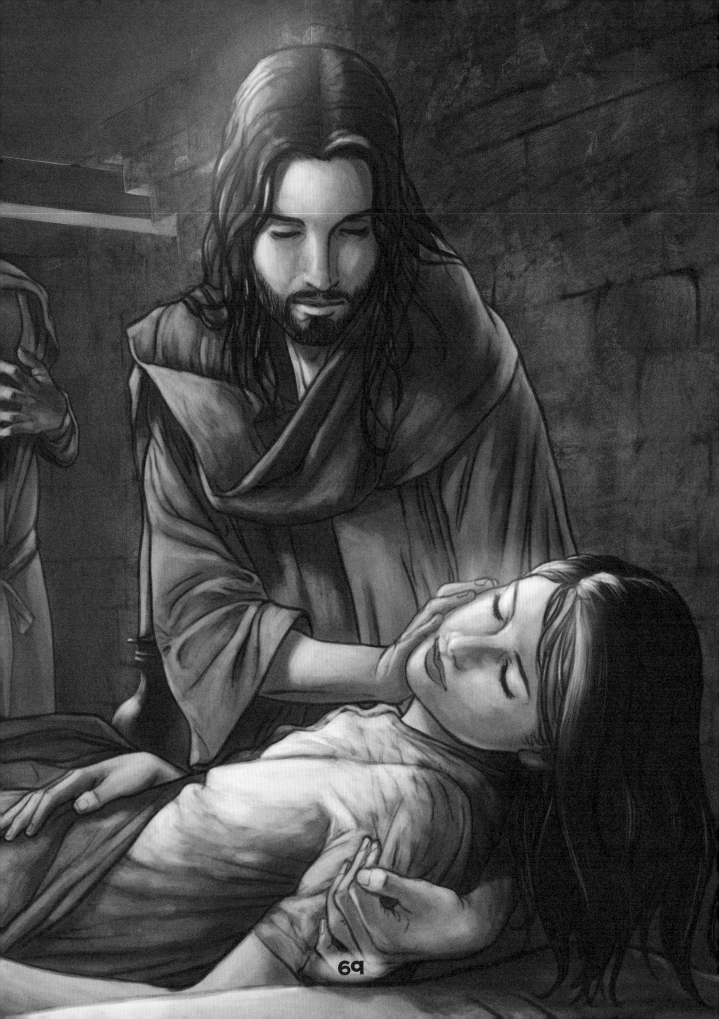

Her parents were so shocked that they did not know what to say. Jesus had brought their little girl back to life. He had raised her from the dead!

They must have hugged her so tightly! And they must have thanked Jesus again and again!

"Give her something to eat," Jesus said kindly. After all, she had not eaten for quite some time.

When Jesus came out of the room, everyone dropped to their knees. They bowed with their faces to the ground. They wanted to worship the Man who had power over death.

"The girl is alive!" the people shouted. Their wailing turned to singing.

They probably had a big party. And Jesus was the guest of honor! They wanted to celebrate the new life that He had given to the girl.

But a greater miracle was yet to come. Jesus would soon give His life on the cross. He would be in a tomb for three days. Then He would be raised to life again.

That would be the greatest miracle of all time!

A Little Lunch

This story is taken from Matthew 14, Mark 6, Luke 9, and *The Desire of Ages*, chapter 39.

Bees buzzed from flower to flower. *Buzz. Buzz. Buzz.*

Seagulls soared along the shore of the Sea of Galilee. *Caw. Caw. Caw.* They hunted for scraps of fish. Sometimes the local fishermen left some behind.

The sun was big and bright. The spring air felt warm.

Jesus sat on the beach with His disciples. From there He could teach the crowds of people gathered on the hills. More than five thousand people had come to hear Him. The stories He told were always interesting. They helped people know God in heaven.

But the disciples were worried. The people had not eaten all day.

"Hungry people can get grumpy," they said. So they went to Jesus.

"Send the people away," they told Him. They thought that if the people would just go away, so would the problem.

But Jesus' mission was to bring people to Him, not to send them away from Him.

He had a better idea. "You give them something to eat," He said to His disciples.

"Feed all these people?" Philip asked. "Where are we going to get enough money to pay for all that food?"

Philip and the rest of the disciples forgot. They forgot that Jesus gave them power to do miracles. They forgot that their loving Savior would not send people away hungry, grumpy, and weak.

Jesus told the disciples to see if anyone had any food to share.

The disciples walked among the crowd. This way and that way they went. Left and right they looked. Here and there they searched.

Finally Andrew stopped in front of a small boy. "Do you have any food that you would be willing to share?" he asked.

"Share my food?" the boy said, smiling up at Andrew. "I guess I could. Are you hungry?"

Andrew must have grinned right back at him. "Well, yes, but it is not for me. Jesus is asking for food to feed the crowd."

"A crowd this size?" The boy almost laughed as he stared into his basket. "I have only five little loaves of bread and two small fish. That is not enough to feed all of these people."

"I would have to agree," Andrew said. "But let's see what Jesus does with it."

Jesus held the boy's basket of food as He prayed. When He finished the blessing, He reached in.

Jesus took out a small loaf of barley bread. He tore it down the middle, breaking it into two pieces. Then He tore both pieces in half again. He did this again, and again, and again! He did the same thing with the fish.

The boy's eyes grew big. "How did He do that?" he asked himself. "I gave Jesus a little food. Now the basket is full!"

Soon everyone was enjoying plenty to eat, including the boy. Jesus had taken his little lunch and made it a lot!

Dark Night

This story is taken from Matthew 26-28, Mark 14-16, Luke 22-24, John 14-21, and *The Desire of Ages*, chapters 74-87.

It was a dark night. Jesus and His disciples walked to the Garden of Gethsemane.

Jesus was very sad. But His disciples did not understand why. They did not know that bad people would soon hurt Jesus. They would bully Him. They would beat Him. They would nail Him to a cross.

In the garden the disciples fell asleep. But Jesus fell on His face in prayer.

"Oh, My Father in heaven," He prayed, "if it is possible, please take this cup of suffering from Me. Nevertheless, not My will, but Yours, be done!"

When Jesus hung on the cross, it was as if the weight of the world was on His shoulders—and it was! The bad things everyone has done were put on Jesus. This good, perfect Man paid the price for our disobedience.

Jesus did not want to die on the cross. But He knew that He had to if He wanted to save us.

Suddenly Jesus cried out, "It is finished!" Then He died.

But He won the battle against Satan. His death made it possible for people to choose eternal life in heaven.

INRI
IESVS NAZARENVS
REX IVDAEORVM

Jesus died on a Friday. His body rested in the tomb over the Sabbath day. But on Sunday morning, something amazing happened.

The ground began to shake. Then a bright flash of light came down from the sky. It shone right on the stone in front of Jesus' tomb.

An angel rolled back the stone. "Son of God, come out!" the angel shouted. "Your Father calls You!"

Other angels came to see this exciting event. Now a choir of angels burst into song to welcome Jesus from the grave!

Jesus stood at the opening of the tomb. No longer was He dressed in the clothes of a poor man. He was in the glorious robes of heaven.

"I am the resurrection and the life!" He said.

Jesus was no longer dead! He had risen just as He said He would.

After His resurrection Jesus visited many people, including His disciples. He spent forty precious days with them. Then He led them to the Mount of Olives.

Jesus was going to go back to heaven.

Before He left, He told the disciples, "Go and make disciples of all nations." He wanted them to spread the good news of His gift of eternal life.

Then He made one last promise to them and to us: "I am with you always, even to the end of the world."

As He blessed them, He began to rise up into heaven. Then two angels appeared. They told the disciples, "This same Jesus will come back in the same way that you saw Him go into heaven."

What a promise! He is coming back for us so we can live with Him in heaven!

BOOKS YOU CAN TRUST!

The History of Freedom

Are you ready to dig deeper into God's word? Are you ready to discover for yourself the truth about the last days?

Your Questions God's Answers

God's answers from the Bible. Is there hope? What will be the signs of the end of the world, and many others.

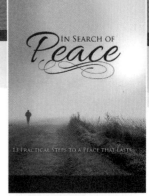

In Search of Peace

An all time best-seller, printed in over 100 languages. Find the answer to problems people are facing like how to achieve freedom from worry, guilt, and fear.

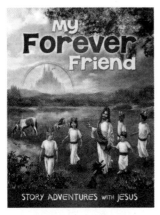

My Forever Friend

Each story from the life of Christ features beautiful artwork and text that will engage your child.

Old Testament Bible Story Adventures

The Bible is full of great stories. Your children will love to read about the faith and courage of God's followers.

New Testament Bible Story Adventures

Jesus is God, but He became a person to that all of us could learn a better way to live. Your children will discover peace and security as they read about Jesus and His love for them.

Give Them Something Better

Beautiful, Delicious, Nutritious, Fresh. That is what every meal should be and can be with this wonderful new resource.

Live Life to the Fullest

Learn to Live – the 8 Essentials of Optimum Health. Choice, rest, environment, activity, trust, interpersonal relationships, outlook and nutrition.

Habits that Heal: Habits from America's Longest Living People

A group of people in Loma Linda, California, are known as one of the world's healthiest longest living people. Discover the secret to their long, healthy lives.

FAMILY HOME CHRISTIAN BOOKS

To order visit: www.FamilyHomeChristianBooks.com
or call now: (800) 4-A-NEW-LIFE (800) 426-3954